SHREK
COOKBOOK

SHREK
COOKBOOK

Contents

The fastest cheese
slicer in town.

Shrek's kitchen rules

Shrek isn't usually a rules kind of guy, but he makes an exception when it comes to cooking. The kitchen can be a dangerous place so follow Shrek's simple rules for a safe, clean, and fun time cooking.

Always ask an adult for help

This is Shrek's **golden** rule: You must always have an adult with you when you're cooking any of the recipes. You will need their help, especially when you are using sharp knives and hot stoves or ovens.

You must be extra careful when you see this symbol.

Unfortunately, slug juice is not one of our recipes.

Think ahead

The best cooks are always prepared. Before you begin cooking, read the recipe through so that you know what to expect. It is also a good idea to find all the ingredients and tools you will need before you start to cook.

Fiona's tips

Always tie long hair back so that it stays out of your face—and out of your food! Wear an apron to protect your clothes or wear something old.

Be clean and tidy

It sounds odd coming from Shrek but always wash your hands before you start cooking and always wash them after touching raw meat. Use separate chopping boards for meat and vegetables. Keep your work area tidy and clean up as you go along for a calmer cooking experience.

Be careful not to singe yourself!

Hot food may be too hot to touch.

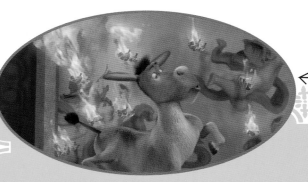

Be sensible, be safe

Follow Shrek's rules for safe and happy cooking. Concentrate on what you are doing at all times or accidents can happen. Most importantly, don't forget to ASK AN ADULT FOR HELP!

If you follow Shrek's rules, you will have a safe and hygienic time in the kitchen, but Gingy has one final piece of advice: RELAX AND HAVE FUN!

The Three Bears' porridge

Ever asked yourself that age-old question, "Who's been eating my porridge?" Well EVERYONE will be if you follow this family recipe from Mother Bear. It's not too hot, not too cold—it's just right. Just keep an eye out for lost little girls—they're notorious porridge-pilferers.

Ingredients

(SERVES 4)

· 2¾ cups rolled oats
· 1¼ cups milk
· 2 bananas (sliced)
· 2–3 tbsp honey

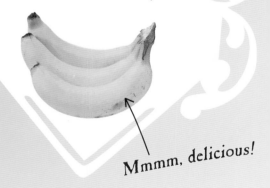

Mmmm, delicious!

⚠ **1.** Place the oats and the milk in a small saucepan and bring them to a boil, stirring frequently so that it doesn't stick.

A great way to start the day!

Being evicted from your home and forced to squat in an ogre's swamp doesn't make for a restful night's sleep! Thank goodness Mother Bear packed the porridge oats before they left home—puréed swamp weeds aren't so appetizing first thing in the morning!

2. After 5–7 minutes, the cooked porridge will have thickened. Carefully take the pan off the heat.

Just right!

3. Pour the porridge into bowls. Top with a little honey and some sliced banana and serve!

Too cold

Too hot

Sleeping Beauty pancakes

These pancakes are a delicious way to start the day after being asleep for a hundred years. And if you've just been woken up by a handsome prince, there's only one drawback—you're going to have to share them with him!

Sleepy head

1. Sift the flour, baking powder, and salt into a mixing bowl. Stir in the sugar with a wooden spoon and set the bowl aside.

2. Crack the egg into a bowl and then add it to the measuring cup containing the milk. Whisk together well.

3. Pour the milk and egg mixture into the flour and beat with a wooden spoon. Fold in the blueberries gently, being careful not to crush them.

4. Melt a quarter of the butter in a large nonstick frying pan over medium heat. When the butter begins to bubble, you are ready to start cooking the pancakes.

5. To make each pancake, place a large spoonful of batter into the pan. Fry for two minutes or until bubbles appear on the top.

Have a nice trip!

No matter where she is or what she's doing, Sleeping Beauty can't help but fall asleep. Sometimes falling asleep at the drop of a hat can be inconvenient and rather embarassing, but it can be quite useful—especially if there are pesky guards to trip up!

6. Flip the pancakes over using a spatula and cook the other side for 2 minutes or until they are cooked through. Repeat with the remaining batter.

7. Serve the pancakes while they are still warm with maple syrup and sliced banana.

Beware of the thorns!

Waffles à la Donkey

He may drive Shrek and Fiona up the wall, but they love it when he makes his morning waffles. They're so tasty they even keep donkey quiet—for a while. Shrek agrees: Donkey certainly knows a lot about waffling!

Ingredients

(SERVES 4)

- 8 frozen waffles
- ½ cup yogurt
- 1 cup raspberries
- Maple syrup for drizzling

1. First you need to heat the waffles. Place them in the toaster in batches or under a medium broiler. Check the instructions on the packaging.

2. Once they are warmed through, take four plates and place two waffles on each of them. Top each waffle with a tablespoon of yogurt and some raspberries and drizzle with a little maple syrup.

An uninvited guest

Donkey has a knack for turning up at Shrek and Fiona's swamp at the most inconvenient times. He may be an uninvited guest but he certainly does make mouthwatering waffles!

"...and in the morning, I'm making waffles!"

Tasty toppings

Although he'll never admit it, Shrek secretly loves waffles, although he'd rather Donkey serve them topped with crystalized caterpillars and drizzled with fish oil! You can serve your waffles with anything you like. Why not try sliced banana with a little chocolate sauce or frozen yogurt with strawberries? Whatever topping you choose it's sure to be tastier than Shrek's fishy favorite!

Easily excited

Sometimes Donkey gets carried away!

Much nicer than crystalized caterpillar!

Magical morning potions

You don't have to be a fairy godmother to concoct these colorful potions. You don't even need a wand: a juicer is much easier and there's less chance of turning yourself into a toad by mistake! Make these juices and you can drink happily ever after.

Ingredients
(EACH RECIPE MAKES 1 GLASS OF JUICE)

Carrot and apple juice:
- 4 apples (washed and stems removed)
- 3 carrots (scrubbed)
- fresh lemon juice

Raspberry and orange juice:
- 2 cups fresh raspberries (washed)
- 4 fresh oranges (peeled)
- fresh lemon juice

Blackberry, blueberry, and apple juice:
- 1¾ cups fresh blackberries (washed)
- ¾ cups fresh blueberries (washed)
- 4 apples (washed and stems removed)
- fresh lemon juice

1. Carefully cut the carrots into small chunks and then slice the apples into quarters.

2. Put the carrot and apple pieces into the juicer and juice them. Discard the pulp and pour the juice into glasses. If you don't have a juicer, use a blender to purée the fruit and then separate the juice from the pulp with a fine strainer.

Be creative!
Fairy Godmother likes to think of weird and wonderful names for her magical potions. Why don't you try and come with some ideas for yours? How about Berry Blaster or Fruit Fancy?

3. Finally, add a little fresh lemon juice. It will preserve the vitamins in the juice and bring out the flavors.

4. To make the other juices, repeat steps 1, 2, and 3 using the appropriate fruits.

Blackberry, blueberry, and apple juice

Carrot and apple juice

Raspberry and orange juice

Merlin's granola crunch

Wise wizards will always tell you that when whipping up a good spell it's all about quality ingredients—best wing of bat, the freshest moonbeams, and so on. The same goes when making breakfast. Merlin conjures up the finest fruits, nuts, and seeds to make this magical munch.

Ingredients

(SERVES 6)

- 1 tbsp olive oil
- 3 tbsp honey
- 4½ cups jumbo rolled oats
- ½ cup Brazil nuts (optional)
- ¼ cup sunflower seeds
- ½ cup dried pineapple pieces
- ½ cup toasted coconut flakes
- ½ cup dried banana chips
- ½ cup dried apricots

1. Preheat the oven to 400°F (200°C). Carefully chop the Brazil nuts into medium sized pieces.

2. Pour the oil and honey into a pan and melt over a low heat. Add the oats, nuts, and sunflower seeds to the pan and stir together well.

Gets you in touch with your inner nut!

3. Take the pan off the heat and spread the mixture on a baking tray and bake in the oven for 10 minutes, or until the mixture begins to turn golden. Spoon the oat clusters onto a plate and leave to cool.

Merlin's top tip

It doesn't take much for Merlin to break out in an itchy rash, so he always pays very close attention to what he eats. If you are allergic to nuts you should leave them out of this recipe. It'll still taste magical without them!

Wizard's cap doubles as chef's hat.

It's healthy and good for your aura!

4. Cut the pineapple chunks and apricots into smaller pieces and break the banana chips in half. Put the fruit in a bowl and mix in the coconut and the oat clusters.

5. Serve the granola with some yogurt or milk in a magical bowl.

Don't spill it on your spell book!

Light lunches &
delicious dinners

Swamp weed and fly larvae

Dips like guacamole and hummus are great when entertaining friends—especially friends like Donkey who are always dipping into your larder anyway. Shrek and Fiona like to serve these dips—made with real weeds and fly larvae of course—then let their guests play "guess the ingredients" after they've eaten them!

Guacamole:

1. Cut the avocadoes in half, working around the pit. Scoop out the pit and then the avocado flesh. Finely chop the flesh and put it into a bowl.

2. Put the onion, garlic, lime juice, tomato, hot sauce, and cilantro in the mixing bowl. Season with salt and pepper and then mix all of the ingredients together.

Ingredien s

(SERVES 6–8)

Guacamole:
- 3 ripe avocadoes
- 1 garlic clove
- ½ red onion (finely diced)
- Juice of 1 lime
- 2 oma oes (seeded and diced)
- Sal and pepper
- 3 bsp chopped fresh cilan ro
- 3–4 dashes ho sauce

Hummus:
- 15oz (400g) can chickpeas
- 3 bsp olive oil
- ½ sp ground cumin
- 2 bsp ahini pas e
- 1 garlic clove (chopped)
- Juice of ½ lemon

Hummus:

1. Empty the can of chickpeas into a strainer or a colander to drain them and then rinse them under cold water.

Slug dippers!
The dips go perfectly with pita bread or crudités. However, they are difficult to get hold of in Shrek's swamp. Luckily, sliced giant slug is a great substitute.

2. Put the chickpeas in the blender or food processor, add the remaining hummus ingredients, and blend them until smooth.

Creamy fly larvae

You might prefer to serve olives instead of eyeballs!

Molten lava soup

What could be better for a fire-breathing dragon than a steaming hot bowl of molten lava soup? If, however, you're a mere human and not so heat-resistant, it's probably wise to stick to soup of the tomato variety!

Ingredients

(SERVES 2–4)

- 1 small onion
- 1 carrot
- 2 tbsp olive oil
- 1 garlic clove (peeled and crushed)
- 1 tbsp flour
- 14oz (400g) can chopped tomatoes
- 1 tbsp tomato paste
- 1 tsp fresh thyme leaves
- 2 cups vegetable stock
- 1 pinch sugar
- 1 squeeze of lemon juice
- Ground black pepper

1. Peel and dice the onion and carrot. Heat the oil in a medium saucepan over a medium heat.

2. Add the onion and carrot to the pan and cook them for about 5 minutes to soften, stirring occasionally. Stir in the garlic and the flour and cook the mixture for 1 minute.

3. Add the tomatoes, tomato paste, stock, sugar, and lemon juice and bring to a boil. Reduce to a simmer and cook for 20–25 minutes. Take the soup off the heat and leave it to cool.

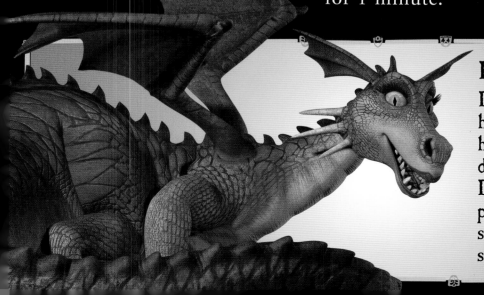

Dragon's top tip

Dragon loves her soup red hot and adds a dash of spicy hot sauce to hers before she devours it, but if, like Donkey, you have a cooler palate, try adding a dollop of sour cream to the bowl of soup just before you eat it.

4. Ladle the soup into a blender, season with pepper, and blend until smooth (warning: make sure the soup is cool to avoid a buildup of steam). Pour the soup back into the pan and bring to a simmer.

5. Ladle the soup into bowls and serve with warm, toasted bread.

Dragon toasts bread with her fiery breath!

Scorch marks are unavoidable if you're a fire-breathing dragon!

Ingredients

(SERVES 2–4)

- 1 cup couscous
- 1 cup vegetable stock (heated)
- ½ red onion (finely chopped)
- ½ cup sliced almonds
- ½ cup dried apricots
- ¼ cup raisins
- 1 tbsp olive oil
- Juice of ½ orange

Speedy couscous salad

This quick and easy couscous is the perfect meal if you receive a last minute invitation to a ball and your fairy godmother can't conjure up something to eat before you go. Just don't add too much onion—you may have to kiss a handsome prince later!

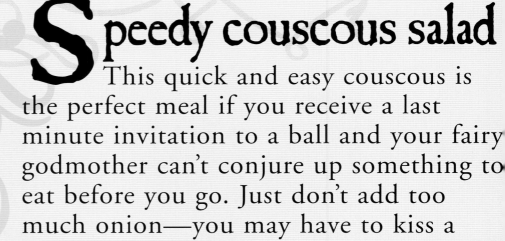

Perfect princess party hair

1. Put the couscous in a bowl, pour the stock over it, and mix together. Cover the bowl with plastic wrap and leave to stand for 5 minutes or until all the liquid has been absorbed.

2. Carefully chop the onion finely and then chop the dried apricots into small pieces.

3. Gently use a fork to fluff the couscous and separate the grains.

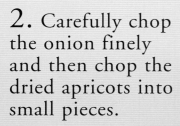

Freshly pressed ball gown →

4. Add the orange juice, chopped onion, apricots, almonds, raisins, and olive oil to the bowl of couscous and mix together.

A princess's work is never done!

Perfect princess

Whether she's having tea with her princess friends or is off to a swanky royal ball, Cinderella is always poised and beautifully presented.

A tasty meal that's ready in minutes leaves lots of time to prepare for the party!

Invitation

Royal Ball

Puss's purrfect frittata

This is a Spanish recipe that Mama Boots taught Puss to make when he was just a little kitten. It's so good, it makes all other frittatas taste like horrible hair balls in comparison!

1. Preheat the broiler to medium-high. Carefully cut the cooked potatoes into small chunks (roughly ½ inch/1cm).

"Do not fear my culinary flair!"

2. Heat the oil in a medium, ovenproof frying pan. Add the diced onion and cook over medium heat until the onion has softened. Add the chopped potatoes and fry for about 6 minutes or until golden.

3. Add the pieces of ham and the peas to the pan and cook for a further 2 minutes.

4. Crack the eggs into a measuring cup and beat them together well. Season the eggs with a little salt and pepper.

5. Add a little more oil to the pan if necessary. Pour the eggs into the pan and cook without stirring for 5 minutes, until the base is set.

6. To cook the top of the frittata, place the frying pan under the broiler and cook for a further 3–5 minutes or until the top has set.

7. Once the frittata is cooked thoroughly, remove the pan from the broiler and leave it to cool slightly before sliding the frittata onto a plate. Serve the frittata with a fresh side salad.

Puss enjoys a slice with a refreshing glass of catnip juice.

The food of love

Puss's cooking skills have always impressed felines of the female variety. Unfortunately he's impressed a few too many señoritas and fur begins to fly during fierce catfights when they all show up for one of his fiestas!

Ingredients

(MAKES 8 FISHCAKES)

- 8oz (250g) potatoes (peeled and chopped)
- Salt and pepper
- 2 tsp chopped fresh parsley
- 12oz (350g) canned tuna (drained weight)
- ¾ cup flour
- 2 tsp Dijon mustard
- 2 eggs (beaten)
- 1 scallion (finely chopped)
- 1½ cups bread crumbs
- 1 cup vegetable oil

To serve:
Lemon or lime
wedges

Captain Hook's fish cakes

This piano-playing pirate seems to know more about tunes than tuna, so no doubt he stole this recipe somewhere on his travels. Try this tasty dish for yourself—you're sure to be hooked!

⚠ **1.** Half-fill the saucepan with water. Add the potatoes and a pinch of salt. Bring the water to a boil and cook for about 12–15 minutes, or until soft.

2. Thoroughly drain the potatoes and put them back in the saucepan. Mash the potatoes and leave them until cool enough to handle in step 4. ⚠

3. Break the tuna into small pieces in a bowl. Stir in the potatoes, mustard, scallion, and parsley until they are all fully mixed in. Add a little salt and pepper.

They're all mine!

Captain Hook would sail the Seven Seas for a plate of these tasty fish cakes. He loves them washed down with a pitcher of grog, He won't share them with anyone, especially Peter Pan! He'd rather walk the plank.

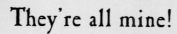

5. Lightly dust your hands with flour and shape the mixture into 8 cakes. Place the fishcakes on a plate, cover with plastic wrap, and chill for 30 minutes.

6. Put the flour and bread crumbs on separate plates. Coat each chilled fish cake in flour, beaten egg, and then bread crumbs.

7. Heat the oil in a deep nonstick pan. Over medium heat, shallow-fry the fish cakes for 2 minutes on each side, or until golden. Put them on a plate lined with paper towels to drain any excess oil.

The Jolly Roger reminds Captain Hook of the good old days.

31

Ingredients

(SERVES 2)

- 6 new potatoes

For the topping:
- 3 tbsp sour cream
- 2 tbsp chopped chives
- 1 cup grated cheddar cheese
- Salt and pepper

For the side salad:
- Lettuce
- Cucumber

Baby baked potatoes

It's hard to imagine a cuter sight than a baby ogre—unless it's these sweet baby baked potatoes. And these babies won't wake you up in the night—unless it's the sound of your tummy rumbling for more.

1. Preheat the oven to 400°F (200°C). Scrub the potatoes in cold water and pat them dry. Prick the potatoes all over with a fork and put them in the oven for ½ hour or until they are soft in the center.

2. While the potatoes are baking, make the side salad by washing the lettuce and seeding and slicing the cucumber.

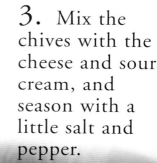

3. Mix the chives with the cheese and sour cream, and season with a little salt and pepper.

4. Once the potatoes are ready, carefully remove them from the oven and cut a cross in the top of each. The potatoes will be hot so be careful!

5. Finally, place a teaspoon of the sour cream mixture in each potato. Serve 3 small potatoes per person with the green salad.

Playtime with Puss

After a tasty dinner the babies love nothing more than to play for a little while before they go to bed. But visitors should beware—although they are undeniably cute, the babies can be a bit of a handful. Turn your back on them for a second and you could end up as their toy!

They're dainty and delicious!

Ingredients

(SERVES 2–4)

For the salsa:
- 1 tsp fresh lime juice
- 1–2 drops of hot sauce
- 2–3 pinches of sugar
- 12 cherry tomatoes (quartered)
- 3 scallions (trimmed and finely chopped)
- Salt and pepper

"I go dippy for dronkey dippers!"

Dronkey dippers

Whether your taste buds fancy something wild or mild, these crunchy tortilla chips and dips are just the thing. Dragon and Donkey never have any trouble getting their kids to come flying when these delicious dippers are on the menu.

Ingredients

(SERVES 2–4)

For the tzatziki:
- 1 tsp fresh lemon juice
- ½ cucumber
- 1 tbsp chopped fresh mint
- Salt and pepper
- 1 garlic clove (crushed)
- 1 cup plain yogurt

For dipping:
- Tortilla chips

1. To make the tzatziki, first remove the seeds from the cucumber using a teaspoon.

2. Next, carefully grate the cucumber into a small bowl.

3. Wrap the cucumber in a clean tea towel and firmly squeeze out any excess moisture.

4. Finally, mix together the grated cucumber, yogurt, lemon juice, mint, and garlic in a bowl and season with salt and pepper.

Dronkey top tip
The dronkies like their salsa really spicy so they add lots of hot sauce—and the results can be dangerous! You can add more or less hot sauce to your salsa to suite your own taste buds!

5. To make the salsa, put all the ingredients for the salsa in a bowl and mix them together.

Fiery tomato salsa

Cool tzatziki

Three Blind Mice melts

This is the perfect snack or light meal for all cheeky cheese-nibblers! The Three Blind Mice squeak with delight when they sink their tiny teeth into these mouthwatering melts. These cheesy snacks are also ideal for pacifying the local farmer's wife if she comes calling with a carving knife.

Ingredients
(MAKES 4)
- 2 bread rolls/English muffins (halved)
- 2 slices of ham (halved)
- Salt and pepper
- A dash of Worcestershire sauce (optional)
- 1 egg (beaten)
- 1½ cups cheddar cheese (grated)

1. Preheat the broiler to medium. Put the grated cheese in a bowl and pour the beaten egg over it.

2. Add a dash of Worcestershire sauce, season with a little salt and pepper, and mix together well.

See how they run!

You should see how the Three Blind Mice run to get their paws on cheese—whatever kind it is. You can use your favorite cheese when you make these melts or try adding fresh herbs such as oregano, thyme, or basil to the cheese mixture.

3. Toast the rolls on both sides, using a broiler or toaster.

4. Place a piece of ham on each roll half and top with the cheese mix. Place them under the broiler until the cheese has melted and is golden.

They taste much nicer than Shrek's ear!

"Three blind mice...

Three blind mice..."

Mouse sense

The Three Blind Mice make up for their lack of sight with amazing senses of taste and smell. They can sniff out these melts from two streets away!

Hey—no nibbling the ingredients!

Ingredients

(SERVES 2–4)

- 8oz (225g) firm tofu
- 1 carrot (peeled)
- 1 red pepper (seeded)
- 2 scallions (trimmed)
- 2 tsp sunflower oil
- 2oz (60g) baby corn
- 2oz (75g) per person, dried medium egg noodles
- ½ cup unsalted cashews (optional)
- 2oz (60g) sugar snap peas

Stir-fry sauce:
- 1 tsp honey
- 1 tsp sesame oil
- 1 tbsp soy sauce
- 2 tbsp sunflower oil
- 1 tbsp fresh orange juice

Stir-fry worms and insects

If you live in a swamp you're never short of scrumptious squirmy stuff to snack on. Of course you have to be an ogre to enjoy it! For those with more sensitive stomachs, try this vegetable and noodle stir-fry—it's delicious and its ingredients are far less likely to crawl away while you're cooking!

⚠ **1.** Half-fill a medium saucepan with water, cover, and bring to a boil.

2. Slice the scallions diagonally. Cut the carrot in half and then into long sticks. Slice the pepper into thin strips and cut the baby corn in half. ⚠

3. For the stir-fry sauce, whisk the honey, orange juice, sesame oil, sunflower oil, and soy sauce in a bowl.

Shrek uses a stick as a toothpick! ←

Crispy creepy-crawlies

Shrek loves stir-fried critters, although the little insects' innards have a habit of getting stuck in his teeth!

4. Heat half the oil in the wok and fry the tofu for 7–8 minutes or until it turns golden. Take it out of the wok and place it on a plate lined with paper towels.

5. Lower the noodles into the boiling water. Bring the water back to a boil and cook the noodles for 4 minutes or as instructed on the package.

6. Use the remaining oil to stir-fry the scallions, carrot, and pepper for 2–3 minutes. Add the corn, cashews, peas, and the sauce. Stir-fry for 2 minutes.

7. Add the cooked tofu and stir-fry for a further 2 minutes. Drain the noodles and serve the stir-fried vegetables and tofu over the noodles.

Fried grasshoppers are nice and crunchy!

Fresh wiggly worms are even more juicy!

Pinocchio's pasta bake

Pinocchio thinks his pasta bake is the the best pasta dish ever—and you know he wooden' tell a lie! Pinocchio's creator used to make this for him when he was little, but he used wood shavings instead of grated cheese!

Ingredients

(SERVES 4)
- 1 large red onion
- 1 clove of garlic
- 13oz (400g) can of chopped tomatoes
- ½ tsp salt
- ½ tsp pepper
- 3 tbsp tomato purée
- 2 tbsp olive oil
- ½ cup water
- 1 tbsp fresh basil (chopped)
- 13oz (400g) dried pasta
- 1¾ cups mozzarella cheese (grated)

1. Preheat the oven to 350°F (180°C). Chop the onion and peel and crush the garlic. Heat the oil in a saucepan over medium heat and fry the onion until it begins to soften. Add the garlic and cook for a further 2 minutes.

2. Add the chopped tomatoes, tomato purée, and basil and season with little salt and pepper. Mix all the ingredients together well and allow the sauce to simmer for about 20 minutes, stirring occasionally.

3. While the pasta sauce is cooking, boil some water in a pan and cook the pasta according to the instructions on the packaging.

Food for friends

This is a real hearty meal for a real boy to share with his friends. Whether they're the type to wolf down their food, make pigs of themselves, or take naughty little nibbles, they'll definitely clear their plates!

4. Once the pasta is cooked, drain it using a colander and pour it into an ovenproof dish. Carefully add the sauce to the pasta and mix it through so that all the pasta is coated.

5. Sprinkle the cheese over the top and place in the oven for 10 minutes or until the cheese has melted.

It's really good, no lie!

Wooden' you like some?

Swamp rat kebabs

Shrek and Fiona's beloved swamp is a magnet for rodents, but if rats aren't so easy to come by or you don't find them quite so appetizing, these lamb kebabs are a tasty alternative!

Ingredients
(MAKES 8 KEBABS)
- 1 lb (500g) lamb cut into 24 1in (2.5cm) cubes
- 1 green pepper (seeded and cubed)
- 1 red onion

Marinade:
- ½ tsp ground cumin
- ½ tsp dried oregano
- ½ tsp ground ginger
- 3 pinches of ground cinnamon
- 1 tbsp chopped fresh cilantro
- Juice of 1 orange
- 1 tbsp honey
- 2 tbsp vegetable oil

1. Mix the marinade ingredients together in a bowl. Stir in the lamb, cover with plastic wrap, and leave to marinate for 1–2 hours in the fridge.

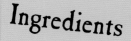

2. Cut the onion in half and then cut each half into four equal wedges. Next, split each wedge in half so you have 16 pieces of onion.

3. Place a cube of lamb onto a skewer, followed by a piece of onion and then pepper. Do the same again and add a piece of lamb at the end. Repeat to make 8 kebabs.

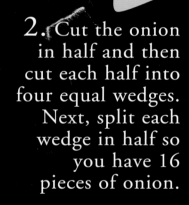

Top tip
If you're using wooden skewers, soak them in water for about 20 minutes before you use them so they won't burn too much under the broiler.

Romantic rats?

Swamp rat might not seem like the most romantic of foods, but for Shrek and Fiona it's a reminder of of their very first meal together, roasting rats over an open fire, while watching the sunset.

⚠ **4.** Preheat the broiler to medium heat. Broil the kebabs for 12–16 minutes turning every 2–3 minutes.

Set the romantic meal off with an earwax candle!

Kebabs go perfectly with couscous! (see p26)

Ingredients

(MAKES 8 WRAPS)

- 4 skinless, boneless chicken breasts (cut into strips)
- 1 small yellow pepper
- 1 small red pepper
- 125g (4oz) snow peas
- 8 flour tortillas
- Juice of ½ lime
- 1 inch (2.5cm) fresh ginger (peeled and grated)
- 2 tbsp honey
- 1 pinch of salt
- 1 tbsp of sunflower oil
- 3–4 dashes of pepper sauce

Renaissance wraps

When Fairy Godmother is feeling blue—possibly her son is having a bad heir-day—she cheers herself up by stuffing her face. Always at the cutting edge of food fashion, she reaches for a wrap because sandwiches are so Dark Ages!

⚠ 1. Preheat the oven to 400°F (200°C). Seed the peppers and slice them into strips.

2. Mix the oil, honey, ginger, pepper sauce, and salt in a bowl. Add the chicken strips and stir until they are completely coated with the mixture.

3. Heat a nonstick frying pan. Add the coated chicken and fry it for 4–5 minutes. The chicken will begin to caramelize and turn golden. ⚠

⚠ 4. Place the tortillas on an ovenproof plate and cover them with foil. Put them in the preheated oven for 6–7 minutes or until they are warmed through.

⚠ 5. Add peppers, snow peas, and lime juice to the chicken. Cook for 4–5 minutes at a medium heat. Stir occasionally to prevent the ingredients from sticking.

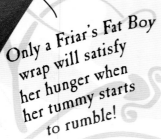

Only a Friar's Fat Boy wrap will satisfy her hunger when her tummy starts to rumble!

6. Lay some of the filling along the center of each tortilla, leaving the bottom and the two sides empty. Be careful not to overfill the tortilla or you will find it hard to wrap.

7. Now it's time to wrap things up! Fold up the bottom of the tortilla and then fold both the sides in.

All wrapped up!

There's nothing Fairy Godmother loves more than a delicious Renaissance wrap. To fulfill her frequent cravings she's tried various spells to conjure one up herself but she's never managed to match the magical flavor of Friar's Fat Boy.

Magic isn't needed to make these wraps taste wonderful!

Ingredients

(SERVES 4)

For the paste:
- 6 scallions (washed)
- 1 garlic clove
- 2in (5cm) piece of fresh ginger
- ¾ oz (20g) fresh cilantro
- 1 tsp of coriander seeds, crushed (optional)
- 2 tsp lemon zest
- 1 tsp lime zest
- 1 tbsp soft dark brown sugar
  2–3 drops hot sauce

For the curry:
- ¾ cups coconut milk
- 2 chicken breasts, skinless and boneless (cubed)
- 4½ cups long-grain rice
- ¾ cup chicken stock
- 4oz (125g) mushrooms (sliced)
- 7½ oz (225g) broccoli (cut into florets)

Swamp slime with maggots

When the pizza-delivery boy has been eaten by trolls, it's always nice for an ogre to know that an easy meal is available just outside his home. This dish is made with fresh swamp slime gathered from just outside Shrek's front door.

1. Peel and chop the ginger. Roughly chop the garlic and coriander. Put all the ingredients for the paste into a blender or food processor and blend until smooth.

2. Place a wok or saucepan over medium heat. Pour in half the coconut milk and half the paste and cook for 1 minute, stirring all the time. Add the chicken and cook for a further 3–4 minutes.

3. Rinse the rice with cold water and put it in a saucepan. Add double the amount of cold water to the rice. Allow the rice to boil. Cover and simmer until all the water is absorbed. If the rice is not cooked, add more water and cook for a few more minutes.

Swamp surprise

Shrek never knows what he'll find when he dredges his swamp for dinner ingredients. The murky depths provide him with an array of tasty morsels like rotten fish, slippery eels, and warty toads!

4. While the rice is cooking, add the rest of the coconut milk and paste to the wok. Pour in the stock, stir, and boil for 1 minute. Reduce the heat and allow to simmer.

Pickled eyeballs provide an extra crunch!

5. Add the mushrooms and cook for 1 minute. Add the broccoli and cook for a further 4–5 minutes. Serve with the rice.

Stagnant swamp water

Swamp gunk

Boiled maggots

Mini eyeball pizza

Here's a lunch that'll really see you through the day—these squishy mozzarella eyeballs are just like the real thing. After he's worked up an appetite terrifying villagers, Cyclops always keep an eye out for this dish.

1. To make the base, mix 3 tbsp of water with the yeast and sugar. Leave it in a warm place for 10 minutes or until it begins to bubble.

2. Sift the flour and salt into a bowl and stir in the yeast mixture. Stir in the oil and then enough of the water to make a soft dough.

He's got his eye on you!

3. Flour the work surface and knead the dough until it becomes smooth and elastic.

4. Put the dough in a greased bowl and cover with plastic wrap. Leave it in a warm place for 1½ hours, until the dough has doubled in size.

Ingredients
(MAKES 4 MINI PIZZAS)

For the base:
- 2 cups flour
- 1 tsp dried yeast
- 1 tsp sugar
- ½ cup water
- ½ tsp salt
- 1 tbsp olive oil and extra for greasing

For the topping:
- 1 tbsp tomato paste
- 13oz (400g) can of chopped tomatoes
- Salt and pepper
- 1 tsp dried oregano
- 1 ball fresh mozzarella (drained and sliced)
- 2 black olives (halved)

5. To make the topping, put the tomatoes into a small saucepan and add the tomato paste, oregano, salt, and pepper. Gently cook over low heat for 2 minutes.

6. Preheat the oven to 425°F (220°C). Knock back the dough by pushing your fist into it and put it on a lightly floured work surface.

7. Divide the dough into 4 equal-sized pieces and shape them into circles, about 4in (10cm) in diameter. Place the pizza bases on a lightly greased baking tray.

Forget to pay your bill at the Poison Apple and you could end up a human candle!

8. To make the "eye" on each pizza, spread some sauce over the base, leaving a small gap around the edge. Place a slice of mozzarella at the center of each pizza and then half an olive on top of it.

9. Bake the pizzas in the oven for about 20–25 minutes or until they are golden.

I spy something tasty!

Artie's awesome burgers

It's a tough break discovering that you have royal responsibilities, especially when you find out that you're newly related to a grumpy ogre! One thing that's sure to raise Artie's spirits is a freshly made burger—a meal fit for a king!

Ingredients

(MAKES 6 BURGERS)
- 1lb (500g) lean ground beef
- ½ small red onion
- 2 tbsp ketchup
- 1 tsp mustard (optional)
- Salt and pepper
- 1 tbsp Worcestershire sauce (optional)
- 1 egg yolk (optional)
- 1 garlic clove (optional)

For the toppings:
- 2 tomatoes (washed)
- Lettuce leaves (washed)
- 6 cheese slices
- 6 burger buns

1. Roughly chop the onion and garlic and finely blend them. Put them in a bowl and add the beef, Worcestershire sauce, ketchup, mustard, and egg yolk.

2. Season with salt and pepper and mix together. It's easiest to start with a spoon and then use your hands to mix everything together well.

A meaty meal

The burgers are a popular choice at lunchtimes with students at Worcestershire Academy. Lancelot and his friends claim the burgers improve their jousting skills—but Artie's never found them helpful...

3. Use your hands to shape the mixture into 6 equal-sized balls. Pat each ball down to make a flat burger shape, ½ inch (1cm) thick. Put the burgers on a plate, cover them with plastic wrap, and chill for 30 minutes in the fridge.

4. Preheat the broiler to medium heat. Place the burgers on a broiler pan and broil them for 6–7 minutes on each side or until they are cooked thoroughly.

Worcestershire Academy miniature banner

Ginger ale

5. While the burgers are cooking, prepare the toppings. Halve the burger buns and thinly slice the tomatoes. Once the burgers are cooked, place the burgers and toppings on a bun and enjoy!

Fiona's feisty chili

This meal really reflects Fiona's personality—it's a dish with a kick! This big bowl of attitude will give your taste buds a good workout. Who knows, it might be you who ends up giving the bowl a good licking!

Ingredients

(SERVES 4)

- 1 large onion
- 1 large red pepper (seeded and cut into bite-sized chunks)
- 14oz (425g) ground beef
- 13oz (400g) can chopped tomatoes
- ½ cup tomato sauce or purée
- 1–2 tsp mild chili powder
- 14oz (425g) can red kidney beans
- 2 tbsp olive oil
- 1 tbsp dark brown sugar
- Black pepper
- Salt

1. Peel the onion and slice it finely. Place a strainer over a bowl and drain the beans.

2. Heat the oil in a saucepan over medium heat. Add the onions and beef, and cook until the onions are soft and the beef is cooked.

3. Add the chopped tomatoes, peppers, brown sugar, purée or sauce, and chili powder and stir.

High-kicking princess!

4. Heat the sauce until it begins to bubble, then turn the heat down low and leave the chili to simmer for about 30 minutes. Stir the chili occasionally to make sure it isn't sticking on the pan.

Hot tip

As an ogre, Fiona can handle heat! If you like your chili hot, try adding more chili powder—but just remember to add a little at a time, and taste it regularly to avoid adding too much!

5. Add the drained beans and a little salt and pepper to the sauce and mix well. Cook for a further 10 minutes until the beans are heated through.

This dish packs a punch!

Gingybread men

You don't need to run as fast as you can to catch these yummy, homemade gingerbread men! But keep a watchful eye on them if any wicked tyrants come visiting—they can never resist snapping off a tasty leg or two.

Ingredients

(MAKES APPROX. 30 BISCUITS)

- 2¾ cups flour
- 1¼ cup soft brown sugar
- 8 tbsp butter (plus extra for greasing)
- 2 tsp ground ginger
- 1 tsp baking soda
- 1 egg (beaten)
- 4 tbsp golden syrup or honey

To decorate:
- tubes of ready made icing (red, white, and blue)
- Lilac gumdrops

1. Put the butter, sugar, and syrup into a saucepan. Stir them gently, over low heat, until they have all melted. Let cool.

2. Sift the flour, ground ginger and baking soda into a mixing bowl. Add the cooled syrup mixture and the beaten egg.

Gingy's top tips

These Gingybread men are perfect for parties, but if you want to save them all for yourself, store them in an airtight container. If you can't find gumdrops you could use raisins or chocolate instead. Finally, don't forget to use the icing to show poor Gingy's injuries.

If you can catch him, you can eat him!

3. Mix everything together until it forms a dough. Shape the dough into a ball, wrap it in plastic wrap, and chill in the fridge for 30 minutes.

4. Preheat the oven to 375°F (190°C). Grease the baking trays with a little of the extra butter and put them to one side.

5. Sprinkle some flour on the table and rolling pin. Then roll the dough out until it is about ¼in (½cm) thick.

6. Press the cookie cutter down firmly and cut out the Gingy shapes. Gather up any leftover dough. Roll it out again and cut out more shapes.

7. Place the shapes on a baking tray and bake them for 10–15 minutes or until they are golden brown.

Have some fun with expressions! Is he happy or sad today?

8. Using a spatula, carefully lift the cookies onto a wire rack to cool. When the cookies are cool, decorate them with icing so they look like just like Gingy!

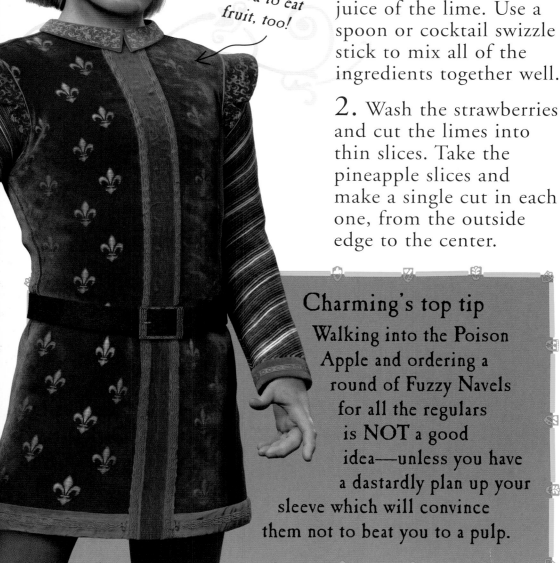

Ingredients

(MAKES APPROX. 4 CUPS)

- 2 cups pineapple juice
- 1½ cups orange juice
- ½ cup sparkling water
- Juice of 1 lime

To garnish:
- 1–2 limes • Strawberries
- Pineapple slices

Fuzzy Navel cocktail

Not many people know this but bad guys just love a fruit cocktail. Maybe it's to replace all the vitamins they lose doing mean things. The infamous Fuzzy Navel cocktail is Prince Charming's drink of choice at the Poison Apple pub.

Bad guys need to eat fruit, too!

1. Pour the pineapple juice, orange juice, and sparkling water into a large jug and add the juice of the lime. Use a spoon or cocktail swizzle stick to mix all of the ingredients together well.

2. Wash the strawberries and cut the limes into thin slices. Take the pineapple slices and make a single cut in each one, from the outside edge to the center.

Charming's top tip

Walking into the Poison Apple and ordering a round of Fuzzy Navels for all the regulars is **NOT** a good idea—unless you have a dastardly plan up your sleeve which will convince them not to beat you to a pulp.

3. Make a garnish for each glass by sliding a strawberry and a slice of lime onto a skewer.

Cocktail shaker

Mabel makes mean cocktails for all her villainous clientele. If Charming is feeling especially adventurous, he'll try Cyclops's favorite cocktail, the Skull Slammer, or Hook's favorite, the Toothless Crocodile.

4. Pour the juice into a serving glass and slide the pineapple onto the side of the glass using the slit you made.

5. Finally, place the skewer containing the strawberry and lime across the top of the glass and add a straw.

Not the scariest looking drink in the world but it does taste good!

59

Marvelous muffins

Do you know the Muffin Man, the Muffin Man? Let's face it, we can't ALL know him, so it makes sense to bake your own tasty muffins. Tuck into these delicious chocolate-chip specials, and you'll feel like you're down on Drury Lane.

Ingredients
(MAKES ABOUT 12 MUFFINS)
- 2½ cups flour
- 1 tbsp baking powder
- ½ tsp salt
- ½ cup sugar
- 1 egg
- 1¼ cups whole milk
- 2 tbsp corn oil or sunflower oil
- 5oz (150g) chocolate chips

1. Preheat the oven to 400°F (200°C). Sift the flour, baking powder, and salt into a large bowl and then stir in the sugar.

2. Crack the egg into a separate bowl and add the oil. Beat the egg and oil until they are light and fluffy. Add the milk and whisk the mixture.

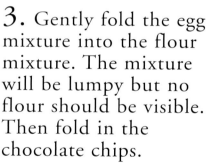

"Do you know the Muffin Man?"

3. Gently fold the egg mixture into the flour mixture. The mixture will be lumpy but no flour should be visible. Then fold in the chocolate chips.

Muffin Man tips
The Muffin Man's famous muffins come in lots of different flavors—try raspberries, strawberries, or blueberries, mixed with chocolate chips or nuts. Delicious!

The Muffin Man baked Gingy!

4. Put some muffin liners into a muffin tin and spoon the mixture equally between them. The easiest way is with a dessert spoon and the back of a teaspoon.

⚠ **5.** Bake the muffins for 25 minutes, or until risen and golden.

⚠ **6.** Remove the muffins from the oven and allow to cool in the muffin tin before placing them on a wire rack.

The Muffin Man has been a busy baker!

Chocolate Chip Muffins

Three Pigs' apple strudel

Nowadays the Big Bad Wolf doesn't visit the Three Little Pigs to huff and puff and blow their house down, but because he loves their apple strudel. Based on an old Bavarian recipe, this sumptuous strudel is the best in the land!

Piggyback champ

"Hey, don't make a pig of yourself, ja?"

Pig in a poke

Ground hog

Ingredients

(SERVES 4–6)

- 4 tbsp unsalted butter
- 2 apples (peeled, cored, and sliced)
- 2 sheets of ready-made filo pastry
- 2 tbsp maple syrup
- 4 tbsp sugar
- Confectioner's sugar to dust

1. Preheat the oven to 425°F (220°C). Place the butter in a pan and melt over medium heat. Add the apple slices and cook until they soften, then add the maple syrup.

2. Lay one sheet of the filo pastry on top of the other. Spread the apple mixture across the bottom pastry, leaving the two side edges and the bottom edge empty.

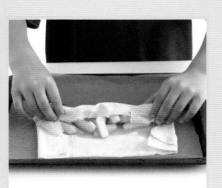

3. Carefully fold up the bottom section of pastry and then fold in the two sides. Now roll up the pastry so it forms a sausage shape.

⚠ 4. Place the pastry on a nonstick baking tray and bake in the oven for 8–10 minutes or until it is crisp and golden. Dust the strudel with the confectioner's sugar and serve warm.

The Pigs' top tip

If the Big Bad Wolf knocks at the door, serve up this strudel and he's sure to eat it instead of you! To make it even more tempting, serve it with a scoop of ice cream.

Some strudel for you-del

Perfect parfait

Want to know something about ogres? They're complex—they have layers. Well, parfait has layers too, but it sure isn't complicated, it's just plain deeelicious! Not only that, but it isn't big or green and it doesn't stomp on people—that's why everyone loves it.

1. Place the mango pieces in a blender. Add the honey and blend until smooth. This is your mango purée.

He has layers—apparently!

2. Put the ground almonds in a small bowl and add the brown sugar. Mix them together well with a small spoon.

Donkey would do anything for some parfait!

3. Take a glass and add a spoonful of yogurt to the bottom of it. Next add a spoonful of the mango purée and sprinkle some ground almonds on top. Continue the layers until the glass is full. Repeat using another glass.

"Everbody loves Parfait!"

Taste sensation

When Donkey and Dragon entertain they always serve parfait because there's a parfait to suit everyone's taste. You can try different fruits such as peaches, raspberries, or strawberries. Delicious!

See? Layers! The ONLY thing ogres and parfait have in common!

Royal chocolate truffles

After a particularly moving performance of his ogre-bashing show, Prince Charming likes to treat himself to his luxury truffles. He has to make them himself—after all, no one's going to buy them for him!

1. Cover a baking tray with parchment paper and then place the dark chocolate in a bowl.

2. Pour the heavy cream into a saucepan and heat on medium heat until it comes to a boil.

My kingdom for a truffle

Manly prince pose

3. Pour the cream over the chocolate and stir with a wooden spoon until all the chocolate and the cream are mixed together thoroughly.

4. Leave the mixture to cool at room temperature. This should take about 1–1½ hours.

5. Once the mixture has set, use a teaspoon to scoop out small pieces and roll them into balls.

6. Place some cocoa on a plate. Roll the balls in the cocoa until they are completely coated and then place them on the baking sheet to set for around an hour.

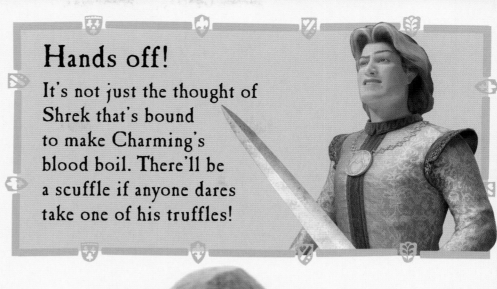

Hands off!

It's not just the thought of Shrek that's bound to make Charming's blood boil. There'll be a scuffle if anyone dares take one of his truffles!

Perfection in confection!

Charming often thinks of his mother as he munches.

Don't stop Believing!

Mommy's little Angel

Ingredients

(MAKES APPROX. 15)

- 2 egg whites
- ½ cup sugar
- 1 cup whipped cream
- Strawberries or fruit of your choice to decorate

Mini meringues

When you're as thin-skinned as Farquaad, it doesn't take much to make you feel small. So the tiny tyrant has come up with a foolproof way of making himself feel big—he's ordered his cooks to make his favorite treat smaller. Farquaad will never be dwarfed by a dessert again!

Now he wants the rest of his meals made smaller!

1. Preheat the oven to 250°F (120°C). Line a baking tray with non-stick baking paper.

2. Put the egg whites into a large mixing bowl. Use an electric mixer to whisk them together until they are light and frothy and form stiff peaks.

3. Add the sugar a little at a time and keep whisking until all the sugar has been mixed into the egg whites and the mixture is thick and glossy.

4. Place small mounds of meringue onto the baking tray, making a little dip in the top of each one. Bake in the oven for about 1 hour, or until they are dry.

5. When the meringues are cooked, carefully place them on a cooling rack and leave them to cool.

6. Once the meringues are cool, top each one with a little whipped cream and some fresh fruit.

Farquaad's fruity advice

Renowned for his fussiness, Farquaad will only eat berries, but other fruits such as kiwi, mango, pineapple, or peach taste great with these meringues!

These mini meringues are massively tasty!

Ingredients

(MAKES 1 PIE)

For the pastry:
- 1¾ cup flour
- 1 pinch of salt
- 9 tbsp unsalted butter (diced)
- 1 egg yolk (beaten with 1 tbsp water)
- 2 tbsp sugar
- 1 egg, beaten (for glazing)

For the filling:
- 1½ lb (750g) apples (peeled, cored, and cut into wedges)
- ½ cup soft light brown sugar
- 1 tsp vanilla extract
- ½ tsp ground cinnamon
- ½ orange (zest and juice)

Non-poisoned apple pie

Poor Snow White hasn't been quite so fond of apples since she munched on a poisoned one and fell into a deep sleep. However, she makes an exception for this scrumptious recipe—although she insists on checking each and every apple first!

1. Sift the flour and salt into a bowl and stir in the sugar. Use a fork to gently stir the diced butter into the flour until it is completely coated.

Mirror, mirror on the wall, who makes the best pie of all?

2. Rub the butter into the flour with your fingertips. When the butter is mixed in, it will look like coarse bread crumbs.

3. Stir in the egg yolk and water until the mixture begins to form pastry. Shape the pastry into a ball.

Snow White's tasty tips

If Snow White suspects that her wicked stepmother has been tampering with the apples again, she uses peaches, raspberries, blackberries, or cherries instead.

"I check my apples very carefully."

4. Wrap the ball in plastic wrap and chill in the fridge for one hour. Flour the work surface and roll the pastry out to about ⅛in (3mm) thick.

5. Preheat the oven to 425°F (220°C). Mix the filling ingredients together in a bowl.

6. Pour the filling into a 9in (20cm) pie plate. Brush water around the edge of the dish and place the rolled-out pastry over it. Trim any excess pastry.

7. Press the edges of the pastry into the plate and crimp with a fork. Brush the pie with egg and make a hole in the center. Bake for 30–35 minutes, or until golden.

Poison-free apples

The Seven Dwarves go mad for Snow White's pies!

Ogre shake

If you blend slug juice, bug eyes, and worm paste you'll end up with something even nicer than chocolate— well that's what baby ogres think anyway. Shrek and Fiona love to see their babies guzzle this gloop—you might like to try his more taste bud–friendly version...

Ingredients

(MAKES 2)
- 1 scoop vanilla ice cream
- 1 tbsp honey
- ½ cup milk
- ¼ cup natural yogurt
- 3oz (85g) chocolate cookies
- 2 tsp cocoa powder

1. Break all the cookies into small pieces and put them in a blender.

2. Next add the honey, milk, yogurt, and ice cream and blend the ingredients for about 1 minute.

3. Once all of the ingredients are blended, the shake should be evenly mixed and creamy. Pour it into tall glasses and serve!

Cute!

Tips for ogre dads

- When burping your babies don't pick up a dronkey by mistake—their fiery burps could burn your house down.
- If stuck for a rainy day activity, earwax makes great crayons for the little ones.
- When happily settled down, don't ignore your old pals—they're the perfect suckers to use as babysitters.

Better out than in!

A great game to play with ogre triplets is to put all three of the little darlings in the bath at once and then watch for the bubbles!
You could play: Guess Who Dealt It, or Name That Stink!

Worm paste makes great froth.

Ogre baby rattle filled with dried wood lice and cockroaches for maximum noise

The babies are as messy as their father!

73

Regal raspberry cheesecake

Smothered in raspberries, this royal treat will make you feel like you're in a fairy tale that's come true. It's light, fluffy, fruity and crumbly but the best part is that it's so easy to make. Make sure you grab the last slice for a perfect happy ending!

Ingredients
(SERVES 6–8)
- 7oz (200g) graham crackers
- 5 tbsp unsalted butter
- ¾ cup cream cheese (at room temperature)
- 1 cup sweetened condensed milk
- 5 tbsp fresh lemon juice
- 2½ cups fresh raspberries

1. Put the graham crackers into a plastic bag. Squeeze out any air and seal the bag. Using a rolling pin, crush the crackers until they are like fine bread crumbs.

2. Melt the butter in a saucepan, over a low heat. Take off the heat and stir in the cracker crumbs so they are completely coated with butter.

3. Put a fluted tart pan with a removable bottom on a baking tray. Pour in the crumb mixture and spread it out with the back of a spoon until it evenly covers the base and sides. Chill in the fridge for 30 minutes.

4. Beat the cream cheese and then add the condensed milk and lemon juice. Whisk them together until the mixture is smooth.

Serve with style!

Royalty are used to the best of everything—whether it's castles or clothes. To make this dessert fit for a queen, serve it on your finest china plates. Queen Lillian loves regal raspberries but you could also use blueberries, strawberries, segments of orange, or slices of kiwi, peach, or nectarine.

5. Scatter the raspberries over the chilled crust base. Pour the filling mixture over them and use a spatula to spread the mixture and smooth it over the top. Chill the cheesecake in the fridge for 2–3 hours or overnight to set.

This fine china is made with real gold leaf!

Frogspawn Jell-O

King Harold hops for joy when he sees this slimy, pondwater Jell-O. It reminds him of happy days as a young tadpole, before things got complicated. Back then life was simple and he didn't have to worry about Fairy Godmothers or cranky ogres marrying his daughter.

Ingredients
(MAKES APPROX. 4)

- 1 3oz (85g) package lemon Jell-O powder
- 4 ripe passion fruit (alternatively you can use ½ cup of raisins, dried cranberries, or milk chocolate chips)

⚠ **1.** Put the Jell-O powder in a glass, heatproof bowl. Prepare the Jell-O according to the instructions on the package. Put in the fridge for about 30 minutes to set a little.

2. If you are using passion fruit, slice each passion fruit in half and use a spoon to scoop the insides out into a bowl. If you're using raisins, cranberries, or chocolate chips, just skip this step.

He dreams of having one last bite of Jell-O before he croaks!

3. When the Jell-O has set a little, add the passion fruit (or the raisins, cranberries, or chocolate chips) and stir. Put the Jell-O into serving bowls and leave them in the fridge to set.

True love

This Jell-O might look yucky but it tastes great. Just follow your heart like Queen Lillian— she knows that looks aren't everything and she loves Harold, warts and all!

Eat it before it hops away!

It's slimy but delicious!

Ingredients
(SERVES 4)

- 2 cups ripe strawberries
- 1 cup ripe raspberries
- 1 cup ripe blueberries
- 4 tbsp fresh orange juice
- 1¼ cup plain yogurt
- 1¼ cup heavy cream
- 2 tbsp confectioner's sugar
- 2 tbsp honey

Beetle juice ripple

Ogres love to eat insects! Shrek and Fiona just adore beetles because they are crunchy on the outside and soft on the inside. This yummy dessert is a bug bonanza—it's filled with oodles of ooze and lots of gruesome goodness.

1. Wash all the fruit. Hull and halve the strawberries. Put the confectioner's sugar, orange juice, and half the fruit in a blender and mix until smooth.

2. Place a strainer over a bowl and strain the blended fruit to remove the seeds. Use a wooden spoon to press the liquid through.

Shrek and Fiona's swamp is teeming with juicy beetles

3. Add the rest of the strawberries, blueberries, and raspberries to the fruit purée and gently stir with a metal spoon. Now you have your beetle juice, complete with fruity bugs!

Shrek and Fiona's top tips

Shrek and Fiona sometimes add grasshoppers to their ripples, but you can add pieces of broken cookies or meringue for an extra crunch. You can try this recipe with any soft fruit, like apricot, mango, or peach.

4. In a large bowl, lightly whip the cream. When it is done, it will stand up in soft peaks. You can use a hand whisk or electric mixer, if you have one.

5. Carefully, fold the yogurt, honey, and fruit mixture into the cream. Take care not to mix everything too much or it won't be a ripple—the cream will just turn pink!

6. Carefully spoon the rippled cream mixture into some serving glasses and enjoy!

You can't beat beetles!

This one got away!

DK

London, New York, Munich,
Melbourne, and Delhi

SENIOR EDITOR Lindsay Kent
U.S. EDITOR John Searcy
SENIOR DESIGNER Guy Harvey
BRAND MANAGER Rob Perry
DTP DESIGNERS Hanna Ländin & Santosh Kumar Ganapathula
PUBLISHING MANAGER Simon Beecroft
CATEGORY PUBLISHER Alex Allan & Siobhan Williamson
PRODUCTION Amy Bennett

PHOTOGRAPHY Dave King
HOME ECONOMIST Mary Luther

First published in the United States in 2007
by DK Publishing
375 Hudson Street
New York, New York 10014

07 08 09 10 11 10 9 8 7 6 5 4 3 2 1

DK books are available at special discounts when purchased in bulk for
sales promotions, premiums, fund-raising, or educational use. For details,
contact: DK Publishing Special Markets, 375 Hudson Street, New York,
New York 10014, or SpecialSales@dk.com

A catalog record for this book is available from the Library of Congress.

ISBN 978-0-7566-2989-2

Reproduced by Icon Reproduction Ltd., UK
Printed and bound by Hung Hing, China

Discover more at
www.dk.com